Anthology 5

William Collins' dream of knowledge for all began with the publication of his first book in 1819. A self-educated mill worker, he not only enriched millions of lives, but also founded a flourishing publishing house. Today, staying true to this spirit, Collins books are packed with inspiration, innovation and practical expertise. They place you at the centre of a world of possibility and give you exactly what you need to explore it.

Collins. Freedom to teach.

Published by Collins
An imprint of HarperCollinsPublishers
The News Building
1 London Bridge Street
London
SE1 9GF

HarperCollinsPublishers
Macken House, 39/40 Mayor Street Upper,
Dublin 1, D01 C9W8, Ireland

Browse the complete Collins catalogue at
www.collins.co.uk

13

ISBN 978-0-00-816048-7

British Library Cataloguing-in-Publication Data
A Catalogue record for this publication is available from the British Library

Publishing Manager: Lizzie Catford
Project Managers: Dawn Booth and Sarah Thomas
Copy editor: Dawn Booth
Cover design and artwork: Amparo Barrera and Lynsey Murray at Davidson Publishing Solutions
Internal design: Davidson Publishing Solutions
Artwork: QBS pp.10, 11, 16, 17, 26, 27, 28, 29, 39, 40, 41, 42, 43, 52, 62, 63, 64, 67, 68

Acknowledgements
The publishers wish to thank the following for permission to reproduce content. Every effort has been made to trace copyright holders and to obtain their permission for the use of copyright materials. The publishers will gladly receive any information enabling them to rectify any error or omission at the first opportunity.

Printed and Bound in the UK using 100% Renewable Electricity at CPI Group (UK) Ltd

An extract on pp.8–9 from *Ruby Redfort – Look Into My Eyes* reprinted by permission of HarperCollins Publishers Ltd © 2011 Lauren Child; An extract on p.12 from *The Chicken Gave it to Me* by Anne Fine, Egmont, 2007. Reproduced by permission of David Higham Associates Ltd; An extract on pp.13–14 from 'The Last Cat' in *Beyond the Stars* reprinted by permission of HarperCollins Publishers Ltd © 2014 Celine Kiernan and two illustrations © 2014 Tatyana Feeney; Two extracts on pp.15–17 from *Robinson Crusoe*, pp.16–24, copyright © 2007 Usborne Publishing Ltd. Reproduced by permission of Usborne Publishing, 83–85 Saffron Hill, London EC1N 8RT, UK. www.usborne.com; The article on pp.20–21 '4-Year-Old Survives 11 Days Alone in Siberian Forest', AFP, 14 August 2014. Reproduced with permission of the publisher; The poem on p.22 'The Shark' by Lord Alfred Douglas, copyright © Literary Executors of the Estate of Lord Alfred Douglas. All rights reserved; The poem on pp.24–25 'Colonel Fazackerley' by Charles Causley, from *I Had a Little Cat – Collected Poems for Children*, Macmillan Children's Books, 2008. Reproduced by permission of David Higham Associates Ltd; Poems on pp.26–27 'Jim Who Ran Away From His Nurse' by Hilaire Belloc, from *Cautionary Verse* and pp.28–29, 'Matilda, Who Told Lies and was Burned to Death' by Hilaire Belloc, from *Cautionary Tales for Children*, copyright © Hilaire Belloc, 1907. Reproduced by permission of PFD, www.pfd.co.uk, on behalf of the Estate of Hilaire Belloc; An extract on pp.33–35 from 'Ice Fairies' in *Beyond the Stars* reprinted by permission of HarperCollins Publishers Ltd © 2014 Siobhàn Parkinson and two illustrations © 2014 Olwyn Whelan; An extract on pp.36–38 from *The Borrowers* by Mary Norton, first published by J.M. Dent and Sons Ltd, copyright © Mary Norton. Reproduced with permission from Aitken Alexander Associates Ltd; An extract on pp.39–44 from *The Kingfisher Book of Fairy Tales* by Vivian French, copyright © Vivian French 2000. Published in 2000 by Kingfisher an imprint of Pan Macmillan, a division of Macmillan Publishers International Limited; An extract on pp.45–46 from *A Midsummer Night's Dream* reprinted by permission of HarperCollins Publishers Ltd © 2014 John Dougherty; An extract on pp.47–48 from *A Midsummer Night's Dream for Kids* by Lois Burdett, Firefly Books Ltd, 1998, pp.40–42. Reproduced by permission of the publisher; An extract on pp.49–51 from *The Lost Gardens* reprinted by permission of HarperCollins Publishers Ltd © 2011 Philip Osment; pp.56–60 *If* reprinted by permission of HarperCollins Publishers Ltd © 2012 Mij Kelly; The poem on p.62 'Hand on the Bridge' by Michael Rosen, copyright © Michael Rosen, 2015. Reproduced by permission of United Agents, www.unitedagents.co.uk, on behalf of the Author; Two extracts on pp.69–72 from *How to be an Ancient Greek* reprinted by permission of HarperCollins Publishers Ltd © 2008 Scoular Anderson; The short story on pp.77–81 'The Golden Turtle' by Gervase Phinn, in *The Golden Turtle and other Tales* reprinted by permission of HarperCollins Publishers Ltd © 2008 Gervase Phinn; An extract on pp.86–88 from *Walter Tull: Footballer, Soldier, Hero* reprinted by permission of HarperCollins Publishers Ltd © 2011 Dan Lyndon

Photos:
p.20 Shutterstock/ID1974; p.21 Shutterstock/Anurak Pongpatimet; p.84 Scott Olsen/Getty Images; p.85 Rick Glase/epa/Corbis

Contents

Anthology 5

Fiction

A Clever Way to Catch a Thief

This is an old tale about a rich man who finds that he is constantly losing things from his house. He suspects that one of his servants may be stealing, but which servant, and how can he be sure to catch the thief?

One evening when it was getting dark and the servants had finished their day's work, he brought them all together.

"Sadly," he said, "we seem to have a thief amongst us, but with your help I think we can rid ourselves of him or her." The servants looked at each other, sorry to think that one of their number was untrustworthy, but uncertain how the rich man could possibly detect the culprit.

"I have placed a table in the centre of the room next door, and on the table is a box. I have put into the box an old cockerel that possesses magic powers. In turn I want each of you to go into the room. It is dark in there, but don't put on any light. Feel your way to the table and gently rest your left hand on the box."

"But what will that show?" asked one of the servants, quite perplexed.

"If you are not the guilty one, nothing will happen – but if you are the thief, the magic cockerel will immediately detect this and will crow so loudly we shall all immediately hear, and know who is to blame."

The servants glanced at each other, some thinking the rich man might be going mad! Other servants were anxious, not sure whether the cockerel really did possess magic powers. What might happen to them, they thought, if left alone in the dark room with the strange creature?

"If you are innocent you have nothing to fear," reassured the rich man.

So, one by one, the servants went into the room, but not a sound was heard. Not once did the magic cockerel crow.

"Excellent!" exclaimed the rich man as the last servant emerged from the dark room. "Now we know for sure who is the guilty person."

The servants were totally puzzled.

"There is a good reason why the cockerel made no sound. There was no cockerel in the box to make a sound! Each of you now show me your left hand. There was no cockerel, but there was soot on top of the box," said the man.

"You," he exclaimed, thrusting his finger towards the only servant with a clean hand, "must be the guilty person. You were the only person frightened to place your hand on top of the box!"

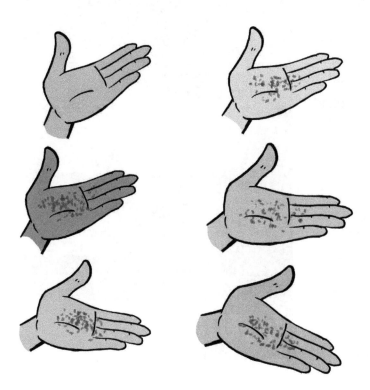

Fiction

From **Ruby Redfort: Look Into My Eyes**
by Lauren Child

There was a girl called Ruby

IT WAS A CRISP OCTOBER DAY in Cedarwood Drive and a two-year-old girl was standing on a high stool in front of a huge picture window. She was watching the leaves fall, studying the patterns they made as they whirled their way through the air. Her eyes followed them until her gaze was caught by a single yellow leaf, almost exactly the shape of a hand. She watched as it swooped down into the yard and then sailed up high over the fence and across the street. She watched as it danced up and down in the breeze and then slapped flat onto the windshield of a passing truck.

The truck pulled up in front of old Mr Pinkerton's grey clapboard house. The driver climbed out, walked up the path and knocked on the door. Mr Pinkerton stepped out onto the porch and the driver produced a map – the two men struck up a conversation.

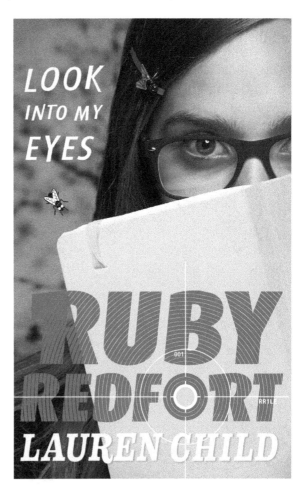

Exactly one minute later an elegant woman turned the corner, carrying a large green picnic basket. With a glance to the house and the slightest nod from the driver, the woman slipped out of her heels, scooped them up and nimbly scaled Mr Pinkerton's fence. Mr Pinkerton was busy studying the map and noticed nothing; the child saw everything. Forty-five seconds passed and the woman reappeared: she was carrying the same basket but it looked much heavier than before and its contents seemed to be moving.

The little girl attempted to grab her parents' attention but since her use of language was still limited she could not get them to understand. She watched as the woman pushed her feet back into her black shoes, walked to the rear of the truck and out of view. Mr Pinkerton chatted on. The girl jumped up and down, pointing at the window. Her parents, sensing she might be eager for a walk, went to put on their coats.

The child drew a truck on her chalkboard.

Her father smiled and patted her on the head.

Meanwhile, the driver folded his map, thanked Mr Pinkerton and returned to his vehicle – waving to him as he drove off. The yellow hand-shaped leaf fluttered to the ground. The woman, now minus the picnic basket, walked on by. She had a fresh scarlet scratch on her left cheek.

The child spelled out the truck's license plate with her alphabet blocks.

Her mother tidied them away and dressed her in a red woollen bobble hat and matching mittens.

The family left the house and strolled down Cedarwood Drive. When they reached the grey clapboard house, the little girl paused to pick up the yellow leaf, and there underneath it, found a small tin badge embossed with an image of something. What was it?

A sudden cry shook the stillness of Cedarwood Drive. A cry that cut right through the heart of the child. She gripped the badge tightly and felt the pin dig into her palm. The neighbours came spilling out onto the street to find the kindly Mr Pinkerton doubled up with grief. Despite the best efforts of the Twinford Crime Investigation Squad – a search which continued for sixteen weeks – Mr Pinkerton's prize-winning Pekinese dog was never seen again.

It was on that October day that the little girl resolved to dispense with the toddler talk and brush up on her language skills. More importantly, that was the day she set her sights on becoming a detective.

The little girl was Ruby Redfort.

Fiction

From **The Adventures of Sherlock Holmes**
by Arthur Conan Doyle

To Sherlock Holmes, she is always **the** woman – the woman who outsmarted him. All my friend has to say is "the woman," and I know who he is talking about. Her name was Irene Adler.

Let me introduce myself: My name is Dr. Watson. Holmes and I shared rooms together on 221B Baker Street until I got married. We lived there as friends for years, with me helping him in his investigations. Later I turned many of those adventures into stories for my readers.

One night, I was walking about London when I found myself on Baker Street. It was March 20, 1888. I looked up and saw Holmes in the second-floor window. I could see his tall, lean figure pacing back and forth. His head was lowered, but I could still see his hawk-like nose and strong chin. He held his hands behind his back. My old friend was hard at work. I hadn't seen him for a long time, so I rang the bell and went in.

Holmes looked at me with his sharp, keen eyes and greeted me with a smile. He seemed relaxed, with his long, bony body stretched out on his favorite old sofa. I found myself at ease again as I breathed in the musty air of his parlor, where we had gone over the details of so many cases together. Then he spoke. "I see you are enjoying marriage, Watson," he said. "I would say you've gained seven and a half pounds since I saw you last. I also see that you have returned to your practice as a medical doctor. I'm sorry you were caught in the rain recently. And equally sorry that you have a careless servant at home."

"My dear Holmes," I said with surprise, "I **have** put on seven pounds since I saw you last. And I was caught in a downpour in the country last Thursday. You are correct in thinking my wife and I are not pleased with the hired help at home. But how on earth did you know?"

"Really? I was sure it was seven and a half," laughed Holmes. "It's simple, Watson. Your shoes reveal they were covered in mud recently. And I can see the scrape marks carelessly left by the person who cleaned those shoes.

"I also detect the faint smell of antiseptic on you, some sort of black powder on your finger that can only be used to treat infections. And there is a bulge in your coat where you normally carry your stethoscope. These clues tell me you are once again a man of medicine."

Fiction

From I Go Chicken-Dippy by Anne Fine

I'd never been outside before. Never in my whole life. I went quite silly, really. I feel a bit of a fool even now, thinking back on it. But I went chicken-dippy. I couldn't handle it at all, not everything at once. Not when the only thing I'd known since I was hatched was wire netting and other chickens.

Try and imagine! First, how it felt. All that wet air and wind. I'd never felt wet air ruffling my feathers before. I'd never even been wet. Now here I was staggering about in a slimy mud puddle, stung by fierce little cold raindrops. It was so wonderful! It was like being born again. I felt I'd come alive!

And the noise! Roaring wind. Creaking tree tops. Deafening! The storm sounded like the world cracking in half, just for me, to wake me after a lifetime of having my ears stuffed with chicken cackle. I wanted to do my bit, so I joined in, clucking and squawking like something quite loopy. Being outside in the fresh air was great.

And it was fresh. Fresh and cold. But what I'd never guessed was how many smells go to make up fresh air. Inside the shed was terrible – terrible! Too awful to describe. At the weekends, when we weren't cleaned out, it was even worse. The workers always wore masks, but even so, on some mornings they coughed and choked, and their eyes were red-rimmed. (Imagine how we felt. We'd been in it all night!) Outside, I smelled a thousand things I couldn't even name until later – the leaf-mould underfoot, wet bracken, a thread of exhaust fumes from the road behind, cow parsnip, smoke from the chimney over the hill, the film of oil on the puddles. A giant stew. Smells of the World! And I was breathing it in for the first time. Me – a bedraggled middle-aged feather baby. But I felt good.

Fiction

From **The Last Cat** by Celine Kiernan

I am not the one in need of playmates,
you understand. The thought of
children makes me shudder.
Grabbish, clutching creatures with
their love of tail pulling – most
of them are beneath contempt.
No, I am not doing this for
myself; I am doing it for the **girl**.
She is the only reason for these
foolish, nightly journeys out
into the cold.

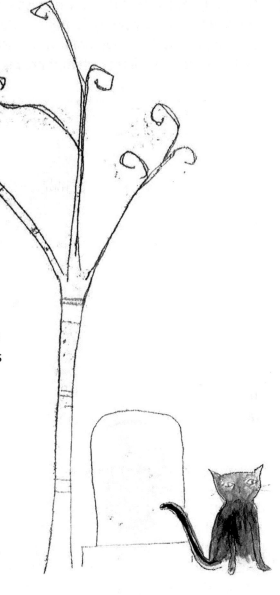

The king does not prevent my
leaving, though I know he would
prefer I stay. This does not surprise me.
The man does nothing these days but sit and
stare into the fire. His people come daily to his
rooms, hoping to rouse him to action; have him
roaring about the battlements, directing soldiers
and firing cannon, as he used to only recently.
But he has given up.

His lack of spirit frightens his people. Without
him, they think they will lose the war. They are
right, but I couldn't care less about their war.
The king's lap is warm, and he is content for
me to stay there as long as I wish – what more
does a cat need from a man? Except perhaps
a morsel or two to eat.

Slim chance of that these days.

The sun has been down for hours, and the air is chilly as I drop from the window on to
the snow-muffled roof. Snow. Bah! No self-respecting cat with even half a brain goes
out in snow if they can help it. It is already almost belly-deep as I pick my way along
the parapets, and it is falling still, drifting like fat feathers from a starless sky. Those
surfaces not snow-covered are already bitter with frost. I have left a warm fire and
velvet-lined lap to be out here. I deserve a medal. Whatever a medal is. Something to be
fondly wished for, if the soldiers are to be believed.

Mind you, I am sure I look very handsome – sleek and black against the white. Certainly I leave very pretty footprints. Perhaps snow is not **too** bad – aesthetically speaking, that is. The footprints will be useful – or I hope they will. I'm not certain what I will do if this latest attempt proves a failure.

The night is peaceful, with nothing to disturb its stillness but the **shush** and **hiss** of the waves at the base of the cliffs, and the whispering fall of snow.

The king's quarters are on the quiet side of the castle – its walls rising straight from the cliffs with nothing beneath them but a dizzying drop to the sea. Despite this, one can clearly hear the cannon fire and screaming that rises daily from the battlefield beyond the courtyards. The noise used to bother the girl. She used to cover her head with a pillow; her mother would encourage her to sing, and so they would attempt to defeat the cacophony of war with nothing but nursery rhymes and hymns. At such times, I was never certain which irritated me more: the soldiers' crashing about or the women's enthusiastic warbling. It was all enough to make one want to jump into the sea.

Ah well, such sounds have not troubled me for a while. These days all is stillness, even during daylight hours – stillness and listening, and besieged humans anxiously peering from watchtowers of burnt stone to the scattered flicker of the campfires on the other side. They are waiting for something; some great final moment that their enemies are constructing beyond the wall. The last explosive step in this hungry war. It will end them all. They are powerless to stop it.

Fiction

From Robinson Crusoe (I) by Daniel Defoe

Robinson Crusoe has been shipwrecked on a remote island.

Eighth day Yesterday I brought back from the ship a quantity of tools, a drill, a dozen hatchets, a grind-stone for sharpening, iron crowbars, a large bag of nails and rivets; with sails, ropes, poles, two barrels of powder, a box of musket balls, seven muskets, a third shotgun, lead, a hammock, a mattress, blankets, clothes and great coats. I thought that I had rescued nearly everything that was on board. But I was wrong, for today, returning from a trip to the wreck that almost cost me dear – the wind having risen, I capsized with my whole load in the middle of the creek – I saw Japp, the captain's dog, come bounding joyfully along, an Irish setter I had thought drowned with the crew. I think that the poor beast, swept away by the current had landed on the island much farther away, and had difficulty in finding me. This evening I pitched a little tent with the poles and sail-cloth, under which I spread my bed. I have piled up all my riches in a shelter from the rain that was threatening. My dog snores at my feet, I have dined on a bit of dried meat and a ship's biscuit, and in spite of a rising wind I am prepared to pass a good night.

From **Robinson Crusoe (2)** by Daniel Defoe

Chapter 3: A new way of life

Crusoe soon got used to life on the island. Every morning, he went hunting with his dog. He shot birds and wild goats for food.

Sometimes he clambered over the cliffs, looking for birds' eggs to cook for breakfast.

One day, while he was out exploring, he made an exciting discovery: ripe ears of corn. He picked them and kept the grain to sow in the spring.

Every lunchtime, he went home and cooked his food over a fire. He skinned the animals he shot, and dried their skins to use later.

The afternoons were very hot, much too hot to work. So, after lunch, Crusoe climbed into a hammock he'd made and snoozed.

After his nap, Crusoe stayed near his tent, making things. When it got dark, he wrote a diary by candlelight.

Time passed quickly. So he wouldn't lose track of it, he made notches on a pole, one every day and a bigger notch on Sundays.

Crusoe explored every part of the island. There was a beautiful valley in the middle, where orange trees grew …

… and lots of wonderful vines, with rich crops of grapes. It was a paradise.

Crusoe began to make friends with the animals, too. He spent hours teaching a young parrot to speak.

One day, he accidentally shot a baby goat. He took it home to nurse and it soon became tame.

Just before the rains came, he planted his grains of corn. The corn grew fast and soon he had a fine cornfield.

But there was a problem. Most of the birds thought the corn looked good, too. Crusoe had to fire his gun into the air, to scare them away.

Crusoe wondered what he should store the corn in. Finally, he decided to make some clay pots.

It wasn't easy. His first pots had very wobbly edges. But Crusoe soon got better at making them. He left the pots to dry in the sun and then baked them in a fire.

Finally, the corn was ready to bake. First, Crusoe ground it into flour. Then he mixed it with water.

He shaped the mixture into loaves and cooked them on a tile over a fire of hot ashes.

LATEST NEWS

MORETON *Weekly*

4 August 2015

Cubs and Brownies to the RESCUE

MORETON: Anglers and conservation volunteers were joined yesterday by Cubs and Brownies from packs in the town to help with the annual spring clean of Prospect Park as part of the RESCUE event.

Moreton Town Council and Friends of Caversham Woods backed the local rivers and environmental clean-up event, along with other local authorities and voluntary groups.

The good news for those taking part was that the volume of rubbish was less than previous years, and down by about half on three years ago when the scheme was launched.

large amount of old engine oil was illegally disposed of in a litter bin which could have caused a pollution accident."

The town's mayor, Mr Jack Alaman, who watched the working parties in the park, commented, "The majority of visitors to our park are proud of our town and its park. They do not leave litter or dump rubbish. But you always seem to get a few who spoil it for the many. I am pleased to see so many young people here to help clean up the park. We seek to involve local schools and youth groups in the care of the area, in the hope that the next generation will care for their environment."

"However, there are still a few local residents who are dumping garden and other refuse within the park," according to a spokeswoman for the environment department at the council. "Recently a

4-Year-Old-Survives 11 Days Alone in Siberian Forest

NEWS *DISCOVERY*

4-Year-Old Survives 11 Days Alone in Siberian Forest

Moscow: A four-year-old girl was recovering in hospital on Wednesday after being lost for nearly two weeks in a bear-infested forest in the Russian far north with only her puppy to defend her.

Karina Chikitova was found emaciated but alive at the weekend, having survived 11 days in the Siberian wilderness in freezing night-time temperatures with only berries to sustain her in what rescuers said was nothing short of a miracle.

The little girl had left her tiny village in the Sakha republic with her dog on July 29 to go and stay with her father who lived in a neighbouring hamlet.

But her father had gone to fight a wildfire and the girl apparently set off by herself into the forest to find him.

With no mobile phone signal in the sparsely populated region where native Yakut people live from hunting and reindeer herding, her mother only realised after four days that her daughter had set off on her own into the dense forest.

Despite a massive search, Karina was still not found for over a week, the breakthrough only coming when her puppy traipsed back to the hamlet in which only eight people live, allowing rescuers to send search dogs on the puppy's trail.

"We were sure that the puppy was next to the little girl all this time, warming her at night and scaring away wild animals," rescuer Afanasiy Nikolayev told the Zvezda TV channel.

A treacherous monster is the Shark
He never makes the least remark.

And when he sees you on the sand,
He doesn't seem to want to land.

He watches you take off your clothes,
And not the least excitement shows.

His eyes do not grow bright or roll,
He has astounding self-control.

He waits till you are quite undrest,
And seems to take no interest.

And when towards the sea you leap,
He looks as if he were asleep.

But when you once get in his range,
His whole demeanour seems to change.

He throws his body right about,
And his true character comes out.

It's no use crying or appealing,
He seems to lose all decent feeling.

After this warning you will wish
To keep clear of this treacherous fish.

His back is black, his stomach white,
He has a very dangerous bite.

Lord Alfred Douglas

Poetry

The Tyger

Tyger Tyger, burning bright,
In the forests of the night;
What immortal hand or eye,
Could frame thy fearful symmetry?

In what distant deeps or skies.
Burnt the fire of thine eyes?
On what wings dare he aspire?
What the hand, dare seize the fire?

And what shoulder, & what art,
Could twist the sinews of thy heart?
And when thy heart began to beat,
What dread hand? & what dread feet?

What the hammer? what the chain,
In what furnace was thy brain?
What the anvil? what dread grasp,
Dare its deadly terrors clasp!

When the stars threw down their spears
And water'd heaven with their tears:
Did he smile his work to see?
Did he who made the Lamb make thee?

Tyger Tyger, burning bright,
In the forests of the night;
What immortal hand or eye,
Could frame thy fearful symmetry?

William Blake

23

Poetry
Colonel Fazackerley

Colonel Fazackerley Butterworth-Toast
Bought an old castle complete with a ghost,
But someone or other forgot to declare
To Colonel Fazack that the spectre was there.

On the very first evening, while waiting to dine,
The Colonel was taking a fine cherry wine,
When the ghost, with a furious flash and a flare,
Shot out of the chimney and shivered, 'Beware!'

Colonel Fazackerley put down his glass
And said, 'My dear fellow, that's really first class!
I just can't conceive how you do it at all.
I imagine you're going to a Fancy Dress Ball?'

At this, the dreaded ghost gave a withering cry.
Said the Colonel (his monocle firm in his eye),
'Now just how do you do it I wish I could think.
Do sit down and tell me, and please have a drink.'

The ghost in his phosphorous cloak gave a roar
And floated about between ceiling and floor.
He walked through a wall and returned through a pane
And backed up the chimney and came down again.

Said the Colonel, 'With laughter I'm feeling quite weak!'
(As tears of merriment ran down his cheek).
'My house-warming party I hope you won't spurn.
You must say you'll come and you'll give us a turn!'

At this, the poor spectre – quite out of his wits –
Proceeded to shake himself almost to bits.
He rattled his chains and he clattered his bones
And he filled the whole castle with mumbles and moans.

But Colonel Fazackerley, just as before,
Was simply delighted and called out, 'Encore!'
At which the ghost vanished, his efforts in vain,
And was never seen at the castle again.

'Oh dear, what a pity!' said Colonel Fazack.
'I don't know his name, so I can't call him back.'
And then with a smile that was hard to define,
Colonel Fazackerley went in to dine.

Charles Causley

Jim Who Ran Away From His Nurse

There was a Boy whose name was Jim;
His Friends were very good to him.
They gave him Tea, and Cakes, and Jam,
And slices of delicious Ham,
And Chocolate with pink inside
And little Tricycles to ride,
And read him Stories through and through,
And even took him to the Zoo—
But there it was the dreadful Fate
Befell him, which I now relate.

You know—or at least you ought to know,
For I have often told you so—
That Children never are allowed
To leave their Nurses in a Crowd;
Now this was Jim's especial Foible,
He ran away when he was able,
And on this inauspicious day
He slipped his hand and ran away!

He hadn't gone a yard when—Bang!
With open Jaws, a lion sprang,
And hungrily began to eat
The Boy: beginning at his feet.
Now, just imagine how it feels
When first your toes and then your heels,
And then by gradual degrees,
Your shins and ankles, calves and knees,
Are slowly eaten, bit by bit.
No wonder Jim detested it!
No wonder that he shouted "Hi!"

The Honest Keeper heard his cry,
Though very fat he almost ran
To help the little gentleman.
"Ponto!" he ordered as he came
(For Ponto was the Lion's name),
"Ponto!" he cried, with angry Frown,
"Let go, Sir! Down, Sir! Put it down!"
The Lion made a sudden stop,
He let the Dainty Morsel drop,
And slunk reluctant to his Cage,
Snarling with Disappointed Rage.
But when he bent him over Jim,
The Honest Keeper's Eyes were dim.
The Lion having reached his Head,
The Miserable Boy was dead!

When Nurse informed his Parents, they
Were more Concerned than I can say:—
His Mother, as She dried her eyes,
Said, "Well—it gives me no surprise,
He would not do as he was told!"
His Father, who was self-controlled,
Bade all the children round attend
To James's miserable end,
And always keep a-hold of Nurse
For fear of finding something worse.

Hilaire Belloc

27

Poetry

Matilda Who Told Lies, and was Burned to Death

Matilda told such Dreadful Lies,
It made one Gasp and Stretch one's Eyes;
Her Aunt, who, from her Earliest Youth,
Had kept a Strict Regard for Truth,
Attempted to Believe Matilda:
The effort very nearly killed her,
And would have done so, had not She
Discovered this Infirmity.
For once, towards the Close of Day,
Matilda, growing tired of play,
And finding she was left alone,
Went tiptoe to the Telephone
And summoned the Immediate Aid
Of London's Noble Fire-Brigade.
Within an hour the Gallant Band
Were pouring in on every hand,
From Putney, Hackney Downs, and Bow.
With Courage high and Hearts a-glow,
They galloped, roaring through the Town,
'Matilda's House is Burning Down!'
Inspired by British Cheers and Loud
Proceeding from the Frenzied Crowd,
They ran their ladders through a score
Of windows on the Ball Room Floor;
And took Peculiar Pains to Souse
The Pictures up and down the House,
Until Matilda's Aunt succeeded
In showing them they were not needed;
And even then she had to pay
To get the Men to go away,
It happened that a few Weeks later
Her Aunt was off to the Theatre
To see that Interesting Play

The Second Mrs. Tanqueray.
She had refused to take her Niece
To hear this Entertaining Piece:
A Deprivation Just and Wise
To Punish her for Telling Lies.
That Night a Fire did break out–
You should have heard Matilda Shout!
You should have heard her Scream and Bawl,
And throw the window up and call
To People passing in the Street–
(The rapidly increasing Heat
Encouraging her to obtain
Their confidence) – but all in vain!
For every time she shouted 'Fire!'
They only answered 'Little Liar!'
And therefore when her Aunt returned,
Matilda, and the House, were Burned.

Hilaire Belloc

Non-fiction

Noisy Neighbour

Environmental Health Department

Southborough Council

High Street, Southborough

Mr J. Trigger
Flat 9
High Risings
Hornsey Lane
Southborough

1 October 2015

Dear Sir,

I fear that we have received yet another complaint from one of your neighbours concerning the noise emanating from your home. This is not the first occasion we have had cause to draw this matter to your attention. I refer to my letters of 29 July and 16 August.

On both occasions you assured me that the problem would cease forthwith, but those promises appear not to have been fulfilled.

The present complaint refers not only to the volume of the music which you, or other members of your family, are playing from early morning until midnight, but also to the sound of your dogs constantly fighting, musical instruments being played at loud volumes and household appliances which I'm informed are in use incessantly.

This letter is our final warning before we shall be forced to take further action to restrain your total disregard for the welfare of your neighbours.

Yours faithfully,

Mr B. Quiet

Complaints Officer

Dear Mr Quiet

I. M. Fedup
5 Hornsey Lane
Southborough

Southborough Environmental Health Department
Southborough Council
High Street
Southborough

Re: Complaint made 22nd June reference no. 654875

8 September 2015

Dear Mr Quiet,

You may recall that I wrote to you previously to complain about
the noise and disruption caused by my neighbour, Mr Trigger.

I am writing to you again to inform you that no improvements
have occurred and in fact the problems caused by Mr Trigger have
become even worse.

Firstly, Mr Trigger and his family insist on playing music
(if it can be described as such) at an extremely loud volume
throughout the day and night, only stopping at midnight on
a weekday. I wonder if all the clocks in their house are broken
because the Trigger family seems to have no regard for the time
whatsoever. This keeps our children awake and our children's
school grades are suffering as a result.

Secondly, the Trigger family has taken on board a new dog. They
now have at least three large dogs living at the house and I am
sure they are the particularly dangerous type. Mrs Turner, from
number 9, is simply petrified and will no longer walk past the
house when she goes to buy her pint of milk and newspaper from
the shop. The dogs are always fighting and barking. Nobody along
the street allows their children to go near the Triggers' house
anymore, for fear of what these brutes might do.

In addition, other constant and extremely loud noises coming from the Trigger house at all hours include the playing of musical instruments and household appliances. The teenage children at the Trigger house have set up a makeshift band rehearsal space in the garage and this entails large groups of unsightly teenagers playing ear-piercingly loud electrical rock music. Even on a Sunday! Mrs Trigger has moved her washing machine and tumble drier into a shed just outside the main house and the vibrations from this are causing cracks in number 7's kitchen wall.

We really are all in despair here at Hornsey Lane. We hope with your position of authority at the Environmental Health Department that you will be able to rectify this terrible situation. Ideally, we would like you to arrange with the Housing Department to move the Trigger family to live in a more rural area, somewhere suited to their activities, and with no neighbours.

Yours sincerely,

I. M. Fedup

Fiction

From Ice Fairies by Siobhán Parkinson

The children came rushing out of school, delighted with
the snowy park. It was thigh high on the littlest ones, and
had drifted deep in corners. The playground was locked,
though. 'Health and safety' a hurried note flapping on
the bars of the gate announced gloomily. But the children
didn't really mind. All the swings and slides had grown
a thick white fur, like static polar bears – only more
glistening – and anyway the icy paths were far
more inviting than playground slides.

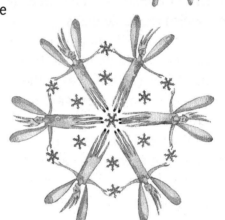

The sky bent low and purplish over the park,
but there would be light enough to play by
for an hour or two yet, the biggest children
informed the youngest ones, who wondered
how it was that larger people always seemed
to know so much: they could even tell
the future, it seemed.

It was one of the very smallest children,
though, who first noticed the fairies in the trees.

"Look," he said, pointing a small damp finger up into
the air – and if you are an older child, which you must be
if you can read this, you have probably noticed that the
fingers of much younger children usually are rather damp,
though there really is no very good reason why they should be,
but there you go, life is full of mysteries.

"Fairies," announced the small child, quite matter-of-factly, as if that was an interesting
enough sort of discovery, but after all only to be expected when the weather
turned cold. For all he knew – he never had experienced snow before – fairies were part
of the package, like frost patterns on the windscreens and water you could walk on.

"Don't be silly," the older children said (practising for being grown-ups), for they
had experienced snowy weather before and knew that fairies were not a weather
phenomenon.

"No, wait, he's right," said a middling-sized child (who happened to be the small boy's
sister, and knew he didn't say silly things – or not much). She was looking where the
small boy was pointing. Brian was his name, but unfortunately he was usually referred to
as Brain at school. "There really **are** fairies."

"Ice fairies," Brain – I mean Brian – explained.

Then all the other children looked up into the trees, and, sure enough, remarkably, every tree, it appeared, was populated by ice fairies. Not even the eldest children, and one or two of them might have been as old as ten – which is double digits, and thus in a different category entirely – not even they could deny that there were indeed fairies in the trees in the park where they played every afternoon and where a fairy had never before been encountered. This was very strange. It might even be a matter that would eventually have to be referred to the grown-ups.

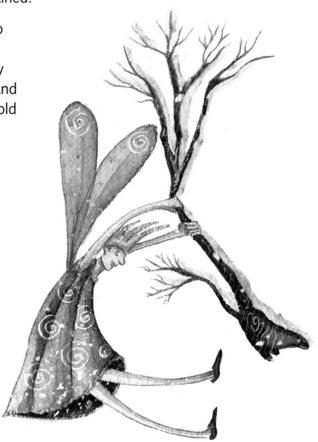

There was a hurried consultation among the double-digit children. The question was this: should they climb up on each other's shoulders and make a human pyramid so the top child could reach the fairies? Bartholomew was for the human pyramid. He'd seen it in books, and he'd always wanted to do it, but he'd never been able to get his friends to cooperate. Here was the perfect opportunity. But Leonora (Brain's sister) said, very sensibly for a child still only in the single digits, that a human pyramid was a dangerous enough prospect in good weather, but could end in broken noses and sprained ankles at **the very LEAST**, she warned, in a very double-digit kind of way, "in these conditions".

"What are conditions?" asked Brain, sucking his finger.

"Weather," said Petronella. "Bad weather."

So then there was an argument about whether snow constituted bad or good weather.

"Good for sliding," said Bartholomew.

"Good for snowflakes," added Petronella, who never could be consistent.

"Good for snowballs," Brain chipped in, taking his finger out of his mouth for a brief moment.

"Bad for driving," observed Petronella, remembering which side she was supposed to be on.

"Bad for feet," said Leonora.

"Feet?" asked several people.

"They get cold," explained Leonora, "and wet."

"Bad for fingers," added Brain, looking at his as if he thought they might freeze up at any moment.

The children's conversation about the nature of snowy weather meandered on. But of course they weren't sitting round a table having this discussion. They were sliding up and down the park paths. They were chucking snowballs at each other and even, in one very sad case, stuffing handfuls of snow down the neck of Brain's jumper. Some of them were standing in the middle of the snow-carpeted lawn with upturned faces and open mouths, hoping it would snow right on to their tongues.

Fiction

From **The Borrowers** by Mary Norton

Kate had sometimes wondered what happens to the little things that go missing. In this extract Mrs May tells her about the Borrowers, tiny people who live in the homes of humans, and borrow what they need to survive.

"I've lost the crochet hook …" (they were making a bed-quilt – in woollen squares; there were thirty still to do), "I know where I put it," she went on hastily; "I put it on the bottom shelf of the book-case just beside my bed."

"On the bottom shelf?" repeated Mrs May, her own needle flicking steadily in the firelight. "Near the floor?"

"Yes," said Kate, "But I looked on the floor. Under the rug. Everywhere. The wool was still there though. Just where I'd left it."

"Oh dear," exclaimed Mrs May lightly, "don't say they're in this house too!"

"That what are?" asked Kate.

"The Borrowers," said Mrs May, and in the half light she seemed to smile.

Kate stared a little fearfully. "Are there such things?" she asked after a moment.

"As what?"

Kate blinked her eyelids. "As people, other people, living in a house who … borrow things?"

36

Mrs May laid down her work. "What do you think?" she asked.

"I don't know," said Kate looking away and pulling hard at her shoe button. "There can't be. And yet" – she raised her head – "and yet sometimes I think there must be."

"Why do you think there must be?" asked Mrs May.

"Because of all the things that disappear. Safety-pins, for instance. Factories go on making safety-pins, and every day people go on buying safety-pins and yet, somehow, there is never a safety-pin just when you want one. Where are they all? Now at this minute? Where do they all go? Take needles," she went on. "All the needles my mother ever bought – there must be hundreds – can't just be lying around this house."

"Not lying about this house, no," agreed Mrs May.

"And all the other things we keep on buying. Again and again and again. Like pencils and match boxes and sealing wax and hair slides and drawing pins and thimbles –"

"And hatpins," put in Mrs May," and blotting-paper."

"Yes, blotting-paper," agreed Kate, "but not hatpins."

"That's where you're wrong," said Mrs May, and she picked up her work again. "There was a reason for hatpins."

Kate stared. "A reason?" she repeated. "I mean – what kind of a reason?"

"Well, there are two reasons really. A hatpin is a very useful weapon and" – Mrs May laughed suddenly – "but it all sounds such nonsense and" – she hesitated – "it was so very long ago!"

"But tell me" said Kate, "tell me how you know about the hatpin. Did you ever see one?"

Mrs May threw her a startled glance.

"Well, yes –" she began.

"Not a hatpin," exclaimed Kate impatiently, "a – what-ever-do-you-call-them, a Borrower?"

Mrs May drew a sharp breath.

"No," she said quickly,"I never saw one."

"But someone else saw one," cried Kate, "and you know about it. I can see you do!"

"Hush," said Mrs May, "no need to shout!" She gazed downwards at the upturned face and then she smiled and her eyes slid away into the distance.

Fiction

The Elves and the Shoemaker
retold by Vivian French

SNIP, SNIP, SNIP. STITCH, STITCH, STITCH. TAP! TAP! TAP!
The shoemaker's shop was very small, but very busy. All day long he snipped and stitched and tapped as he made boots and shoes and slippers. His wife swept and tidied round him and she sang as she worked. They were happy together, and promised each other that the shoes they sold would always be very good, and very cheap. "We can't let men and women and children go barefoot for the sake of a penny of two," said the shoemaker, and his wife agreed.

SNIP, SNIP … STITCH, STITCH … TAP! TAP!
As the weeks and months and years went by the shoemaker and his wife grew older and poorer and hungrier. Their shop was small, and the people of the town forgot it was there and went to buy their boots and shoes at the big new town over the hill.

"Should we move to the big town ourselves?" asked the shoemaker's wife.

The shoemaker shook his head. "This is our home," he said, "and tomorrow is another day. Our shoes are very good and very cheap. I'm sure things will get better."

SNIP … STITCH … TAP!
Things did not get better. They got much worse, and at last there were no pennies left and nothing at all in the kitchen cupboard.

"I have just enough leather to make one last pair of shoes," the shoemaker said. "I will cut them tonight, and tomorrow I will make them."

"And after that?" said his wife.

The shoemaker patted her arm.

"Tomorrow is another day," he said. But neither he nor his wife slept very well that night.

BONG! BONG! BONG! BONG! BONG! BONG!

The church clock struck six and the shoemaker got up to make the last pair of shoes. He went sadly down the stairs to his shop – but he stopped in the doorway in amazement. There, on the table, was a wonderful pair of shoes, made from the leather he had cut out the night before. The shoemaker rubbed his eyes, but the shoes did not disappear. He picked them up and took them to the window to look at them. They were perfectly made, with the tiniest of stitches. The shoemaker called for his wife, and she came hurrying in to stare as well.

BANG! BANG! BANG!

Someone was knocking at the door of the shop. The shoemaker's wife opened the door and a man in a suit of the finest velvet came striding in.

"Good morning! Good morning!" he said. "What a wonderful pair of shoes! They're exactly what I'm looking for! May I ask how much they cost?"

The shoemaker and his wife looked at each other. They didn't know what to say. The man in the velvet suit pulled a purse from his pocket.

"Here!" he said. "Such a magnificent pair of shoes deserves a magnificent price!" And he handed the shoemaker the purse, took the shoes and strode out of the shop.

"Well I never!" said the shoemaker.

"Fancy that!" said his wife, and she emptied the purse on the table. "Oh, Shoemaker! Look! So much money!"

JINGLE! JINGLE! JINGLE!

The shoemaker shook the purse as he walked along the road to the market. He had enough money to buy leather to make two pairs of shoes. There was even enough to buy bread and cheese.

That afternoon the shoemaker smiled as he cut the leather, and his wife hummed as she swept up the cuttings and leavings.

"I'll make the shoes tomorrow morning," the shoemaker said. "Tonight we'll have a good supper!"

"Indeed we will," said his wife, and she gave the shoemaker a kiss.

BONG! BONG! BONG! BONG! BONG! BONG! The shoemaker got up the next morning as the church clock struck. He went downstairs to his shop – and again he stopped and stared. There, on the table, were two pairs of shoes. They were beautiful shoes, beautifully stitched – and made from the leather the shoemaker had cut out the night before.

"Wife!" called the shoemaker. "Wife! Quick! Come and see!" And his wife came hurrying in to stare.

BANG! BANG! BANG!
Someone was knocking at the door of the shop. The shoemaker's wife opened the door, and in came two grand ladies dressed in satins and silks.

"What delightful shoes!" they said, clapping their hands. "We must have them!" And they tossed a handful of gold coins onto the table, picked up the shoes, and sailed out onto the street.

"Well I never!" said the shoemaker.

"Fancy that!" said his wife, and she scooped up the coins and counted them out. "Shoemaker! Shoemaker! If this goes on we'll be eating supper every single night!"

JINGLE! JINGLE! JINGLE!
The shoemaker shook the coins in his pocket as he walked along the road to the market. He bought enough leather for four pairs of shoes, and meat and potatoes besides.

He sat in his shop that afternoon, cutting and cutting. His wife sang as she swept up the bits and pieces all around him. The shoemaker yawned as he put his scissors down.

"I'll make the shoes tomorrow," he said.

His wife gave him a hug. "Meat stew tonight," she said.

41

BONG! BONG! BONG! BONG! BONG! BONG!
The next morning the shoemaker found four pairs of shoes on the table. As he peered at them, the old shoemaker saw that each pair was stitched with the same tiny stitches.

"They're better than anything I've ever made," he said to his wife. "Why, there's not a single mistake. They're perfect shoes!"

"So they are, my dear," said his wife, "but then it was you that cut out the leather."

BANG! BANG! BANG!
When the shoemaker's wife opened the shop door there was a queue outside. The four pairs of shoes were sold in minutes, and a heap of gold and silver coins left on the table.

"Well I never!" said the shoemaker.

"Fancy that!" said his wife, and she poured the coins into the shoemaker's pockets. "You'd better be off to the market, my dear. Perhaps you could buy me a new broom. My old one is worn out." And she waved the shoemaker goodbye as he went on his way.

SNIP, SNIP, SNIP, SNIP, SNIP, SNIP.
From that day on the shoemaker and his wife became richer and richer. Every day the shoemaker carefully cut out the leather – eight, sixteen, thirty-two pairs – and the next morning he and his wife would find the finished boots or slippers neatly lined up on the table. Their fame spread, and once again the men and women and children of the town came to buy – and so did the people from the big town over the hill.

BANG! BANG! BANG!
Every morning the queue at the shoemaker's door grew longer. It was very nearly Christmas and everyone was wanting new shoes. The shoemaker was as busy as he had ever been, and his wife sang all day long. One afternoon, however, she stopped and leant on her broom.

"Shoemaker," she said, "I've been thinking. All these months someone has been helping us. Someone has been stitching and sewing the shoes we sell, and they've never had a penny or a thank you. Why don't we watch and see who it is?"

The shoemaker put down his scissors. "You're right, Wife," he said. "We'll watch tonight."

TIPTOE, TIPTOE, TIPTOE.
That night the shoemaker and his wife crept into the shop and hid themselves behind an old curtain. The pieces of leather for the next day's shoes were on the table, just as usual.

"I wonder who will come?" whispered the shoemaker.

"Shh!" said his wife. She had heard a little noise.
PATTER, PATTER, PATTER!

As the shoemaker and his wife peeped around the curtain, two little elves came skipping into the room. They hopped up onto the table and sat stitching and sewing the whole night long. The shoemaker and his wife watched with wide eyes. As the morning sun came beaming through the window, the elves yawned, stretched and hopped off the table and away. Every last shoe was finished, stitched and sewn to perfection.

"WELL I NEVER!" exclaimed the shoemaker.

"FANCY THAT!" said his wife. "And the poor little things wearing nothing but rags!"

The shoemaker stood up, and picked up one of the shoes.

"Those little elves have done a lot for us, Wife," he said. "It's right that we should thank them. If you will make them shirts and trousers, I will make them shoes and belts to match."

His wife agreed at once and went to fetch her sewing needles. She cut up a handkerchief of finest lawn and made two tiny shirts. She used pieces of green and red velvet to make two tiny pairs of trousers and two tiny jackets. She found a wisp of the softest lamb's wool and knitted two pairs of snow-white stockings.

The shoemaker hunted through the box of scraps for the thinnest, silkiest leather he could find. He made two little belts of leather, and two tiny pairs of bright red boots. He spent all day stitching them with the tiniest of stitches, until at last they were ready. The shoemaker put them on the table with the clothes, and then, as soon as it was dark, he and his wife hid once more.

PATTER, PATTER, PATTER!
The two elves came skipping and scampering into the shop. Up onto the table they hopped – and then stopped and stared.

"Trousers of velvet! And jackets! And boots!' they called out, and their voices were as small and as high as a bat's whistle. They clapped their hands and laughed and pulled on the clothes as fast as they could. When they were quite dressed they pranced and danced and bowed to each other.

"So fine we are, so fine are we, that gentlemen we both will be!" they said. And they bowed once more, jumped off the table and danced away.

The shoemaker and his wife never saw the elves again. The shoemaker made boots and shoes and slippers all by himself, but now his stitching was as small and neat as that of the elves. His wife went on singing as she swept. Good luck stayed with them and there was always a queue outside the shoemaker's shop.

SNIP, SNIP, SNIP. STITCH, STITCH, STITCH. TAP! TAP! TAP!
The shoemaker's shop was very small, but it was very busy …

Fiction

From **A Midsummer Night's Dream** by John Dougherty

Queen Titania couldn't believe her eyes. Never had she seen such an enchanting creature. "Are you a fairy, or of human kind?" she asked.

The creature made no reply, but carried on staring bemusedly into the woods.

Human, then, since it can't see me, she thought, gazing upon it with wonder and admiration. She circled it, admiring the roundness of its belly; the long curve of its nose; the hairiness of its ears. Once she was behind it, she made herself visible to human eyes.

"Hello," she said softy.

Bottom turned, and jumped with surprise. Before him stood a beautiful lady, dressed in a gown of rich and shining silk. On her head sat a small crown which seemed to have been made out of silver flowers. She was clearly a noble lady, and she was smiling at him in a way that no other noble lady had ever smiled at him before.

"What's your name?" she asked.

"Er ... Bottom," said Bottom.

Queen Titania gasped. It seemed to her that she'd never heard such a beautiful name. "Bottom!" she said. "Never have I seen such a lovely Bottom. You must be the handsomest Bottom in the world. And from now on, you will be **my** Bottom!"

"Er ... right," said Bottom, wondering what was going on.

Titania stepped forward and stroked Bottom's nose. It felt a bit tickly, in a nice sort of way. "I'll order my servants to obey you!" she said. "And they'll bring you anything you ask for!"

Bottom still didn't quite understand what was going on, but the idea of being brought anything he asked for was very appealing.

"Um … Got any pancakes?" he said.

Puck had seen enough. He slipped away to find Oberon.

The king wasn't far off. "Well, Puck?" he said, as his servant appeared. "What news do you have for me?"

"You should've been there, boss! The queen's in love with a monster!" As Oberon's brow wrinkled in amused puzzlement, Puck explained: "I found a crew of daft Athenians practising a play in the woods, and the daftest one of all – well, I couldn't resist it. When he stepped out of sight of the others, I gave him …" Almost overwhelmed by a fit of the giggles, Puck took a deep breath, and tried again: "I gave him a donkey's head! And … then the queen woke up and … and … **and fell in love with him!**"

A Midsummer Night's Dream for Kids

What followed next was hard to conceive;
His friends saw a sight they could not believe.
When Bottom returned, he had a new head,
No longer a man's, but a donkey's instead!
They all trembled with fear and stared at his face,
"Oh monstrous! Oh strange! Let us fly this place!"
The scene that followed was complete disarray;
They howled in terror, and all ran away.
Nick Bottom looked puzzled, "Why did they flee?
This is to make an ass of me!
I'll show them that I have no fear,
I'll march and sing out, loud and clear."
Titania was sleeping in her flowery bed,
When Bottom appeared, his arms outspread,
"Hee haw! Hee haw!" was his ludicrous tune.
Her eyes flew open. She wanted to swoon,
"Mine ear is much enamoured of thy strain.
I pray thee gentle mortal, sing again.
I am enchanted by your lovely notes;
Come, fairy servants, bring him some oats."

She wrapped sweet roses in his hair,
"You are beautiful, beyond compare!
Stay with me forever, I propose."
And then she kissed his soft, wet nose.
Puck was delighted with the success of his plan,
And left Nick Bottom, part burro, part man.
Back to his master, he flew in a dash,
Intent to deliver the latest news flash.
Oberon was eager to hear of the trick,
"How did it go, Puck? Who did she pick?"
"Wait till I tell you," Puck said with pride,
"I know you will be satisfied!
She's in love with a monster," was Puck's report.
"A donkey!" he cried, "to make a long story short."
Oberon chuckled, "What a surprise!
This falls out better than I could devise."

adapted by Lois Burdett

From **The Lost Gardens** by Phil Osment

This play is set in a restored garden at the beginning of the 21st century, and then in the same garden at the beginning of the 20th century.

SCENE 1

(An Old Lady sits sleeping in a wheelchair.)

(Sound effect: birds singing)

MAYA: (offstage) Jack! Through here.

JACK: (offstage) Where are you?

MAYA: (offstage) Over here.

(Maya enters and sees the Old Lady.)

OLD LADY: (waking) Ahhhh! There you are at last.

MAYA: Pardon?

OLD LADY: I've been waiting for you. Where are your friends? Jack and Emmy? Do you like the gardens? You know in the old days there were plants from all over the world here? People used to come especially to look at them.

MAYA: Yes, Miss Dickinson told us.

OLD LADY: But then the gardeners left and the family who owned the house moved away and the gardens were forgotten.

(Jack enters holding a map of the gardens.)

JACK: I think we've lost her.

OLD LADY: Ah, there you are, Jack.

(Jack looks up, surprised.)

MAYA: How do you know our names?

OLD LADY: I know everything. You're here with your school to look at the lost gardens. Now isn't it time you went and found the tropical garden?

JACK: What tropical garden?

OLD LADY: It's through there.

JACK: It's not on the map.

OLD LADY: That's because it hasn't been found yet.

(Emmy enters)

EMMY: You're in trouble. We're not supposed to go off on our own.

OLD LADY: Ah, here she is.

EMMY: Who's she?

(The other two shrug.)

EMMY: She must live in the big house. It's a home for old people. Miss Dickinson said. She looks ancient.

MAYA: That's rude.

OLD LADY: That's all right, my dear. You're having a difficult time at the moment, aren't you Emmy? Anyway, I am ancient. It's true. Now the tropical garden's waiting for you. It's just the other side of the brambles. It used to be called the jungle.

EMMY: Cool.

JACK: It's not on the map.

OLD LADY: Where's your spirit of adventure? Now, you'll need this. There's a gate.

(She hands Jack a huge rusty key.)

OLD LADY: Go on. Take it.

(Jack takes it.)

OLD LADY: It's that way.

JACK: Thanks. Come on, Maya.

MAYA: Goodbye.

(Jack and Maya start to go.)

OLD LADY: But you can't leave without Emmy.

JACK: Oh … well …

OLD LADY: Yes?

MAYA: She doesn't really like the same games as us.

EMMY: Yes I do.

OLD LADY: Take her with you.

EMMY: I don't want to spoil their fun.

OLD LADY: You have to stay together.

(Jack looks at Maya. She shrugs.)

JACK: OK. Come on, Emmy.

OLD LADY: Goodbye, my dears. Be careful of the brambles.

(They go. The Old Lady sleeps.)

If you can keep your head when all about you
Are losing theirs and blaming it on you;
If you can trust yourself when all men doubt you,
But make allowance for their doubting too;
If you can wait and not be tired by waiting,
Or, being lied about, don't deal in lies,
Or being hated don't give way to hating,
And yet don't look too good, nor talk too wise:

If you can dream – and not make dreams your master;
If you can think – and not make thoughts your aim,
If you can meet with Triumph and Disaster
And treat those two impostors just the same:.
If you can bear to hear the truth you've spoken
Twisted by knaves to make a trap for fools,
Or watch the things you gave your life to, broken,
And stoop and build' em up with worn-out tools:

If you can make one heap of all your winnings
And risk it on one turn of pitch-and-toss,
And lose, and start again at your beginnings,
And never breathe a word about your loss:
If you can force your heart and nerve and sinew
To serve your turn long after they are gone,
And so hold on when there is nothing in you
Except the Will which says to them: "Hold on!"

If you can talk with crowds and keep your virtue,
Or walk with Kings – nor lose the common touch,
If neither foes nor loving friends can hurt you,
If all men count with you, but none too much:
If you can fill the unforgiving minute
With sixty seconds' worth of distance run,
Yours is the Earth and everything that's in it,
And – which is more – you'll be a Man, my son!

Rudyard Kipling

Poetry

A Smuggler's Song

If you wake at midnight and hear a horse's feet,
Don't go drawing back the blind, or looking at the street,
Them that ask no questions isn't told a lie.
Watch the wall, my darling, while the Gentlemen go by!
Five and twenty ponies,
Trotting through the dark –
Brandy for the Parson,
'Baccy for the Clerk;
Laces for the lady; letters for a spy,
And watch the wall, my darling, while the Gentlemen go by!

Running round the woodlump if you chance to find
Little barrels, roped and tarred, all full of brandy-wine;
Don't you shout to come back and look, nor take 'em for your play.
Put the brushwood back again – and they'll be gone next day!

If you see the stable-door setting wide open;
If you see a tired horse **lying** down inside;
If your mother mends a coat cut about and tore;
If the lining's wet and warm – don't you ask no more!

If you meet King George's men, dressed in blue and red,
You be careful what you say, and mindful what is said.
If they call you 'pretty maid', and chuck you 'neath the chin,
Don't you tell where no one is, nor yet where no one's been!

Knocks and footsteps round the house – whistles after dark –
You've no call for running out till the house-dogs bark.
Trusty's here and Pincher's here, and see how dumb they lie –
They don't fret to follow when the Gentlemen go by!

If you do as you've been told, likely there's a chance,
You'll be given a dainty doll, all the way from France,
With a cap of Valenciennes, and a velvet hood –
A present from the Gentlemen, along o' being good!
Five and twenty ponies,
Trotting through the dark –
Brandy for the Parson,
'Baccy for the Clerk.
Them that asks no questions isn't told a lie –
Watch the wall, my darling, while the Gentlemen go by!

Rudyard Kipling

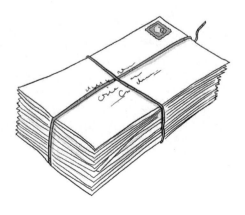

If you can keep your head when alligators
are stealing all the bedclothes from your bed
and keep your cool when, 15 minutes later,
a greedy hippo eats your eggy bread …

If you can walk to school with your big brother
although he really is a dreadful sight,
and wave goodbye, although your lovely mother
has turned into a monster overnight …

If you can cross the playground in the morning –
a playground full of fearsome dinosaurs –
and keep on walking when, without a warning,
they raise their heads and roar and roar and roar …

If you can grin and bear it when your teacher,
who really is a dragon through and through,
tells you to sit beside a toothy creature
who must have just escaped from Scary Zoo …

If you can lend your ruler – though he chews it –
if you can let him use your felt-tip pens,
if you can lend a hand – although he'll bruise it –
and treat him just like any other friend …

If you can eat the food served up by mummies
with trolls and lizards in the dinner hall,
and when the others groan and hold their tummies
say, "Actually, that wasn't bad at all …"

57

If you can stand and watch a spaceship landing
and when the others run away in fright,
you treat the strange green men with understanding
and though they're rude, you are still polite …

If you can count to ten while angry rhinos
are grunting (just because they can't do sums)
and say, "I'll teach you everything that I know
but quick – before the dragon teacher comes …"

And then, if you can play your new recorder
up there, on stage – you're feeling rather stressed
– and all around there's panic and disorder
but you still try to do your very best …

58

If you can play at baseball with a cheetah
who, fast as lightning, runs from base to base
and even though you know you'll never beat her,
you somehow keep a smile upon your face,

If you can run, though others can run faster,
and cheer the winner, "Hip-hip-hip hooray!"
if you can try to stop a near-disaster,
although you'd really rather run away …

If you can keep your head when all about you
are losing theirs and blaming it on you,
if you can let them fight it out without you,
if everyone's a monster, but not you …

If you then meet a tearful pirate fairy
and kindly help her up from off the ground
and wonder how the world can be this scary
and stop and think … and turn … and look around …

Then you will see that they're just human beings
with hopes and worries much the same as you.
Despite their snatch and grab and disagreeing
there's lots of lovely things they also do.

If you can see all this and never doubt it
(though crocodiles will eat your cheesy snack)
you'll love this world and everything about it
and – what is more – the world will love you back.

Everyone's a monster

We're all human beings

Mij Kelly

oetry

From a Railway Carriage

Faster than fairies, faster than witches,
Bridges and houses, hedges and ditches;
And charging along like troops in a battle,
All through the meadows the horses and cattle;
All of the sights of the hill and the plain
Fly as thick as driving rain;
And ever again, in the wink of an eye,
Painted stations whistle by.

Here is a child who clambers and scrambles,
All by himself and gathering brambles;
Here is a tramp who stands and gazes;
And there is a green for stringing the daisies!
Here is a cart run away in the road
Lumping along with a man and a load;
And here is a mill and there is a river;
Each a glimpse and gone for ever!

Robert Louis Stevenson

Hand on the Bridge

Hand on the bridge,
Feel the rhythm of the train.
Hand on the window
Feel the rhythm of the rain.
Hand on your throat
Feel the rhythm of your talk
Hand on your leg
Feel the rhythm of your walk
Hand in the sea
Feel the rhythm of the tide
Hand on your heart
Feel the rhythm inside
Hand on the rhythm
Feel the rhythm of the rhyme
Hand on your life
Feel the rhythm of time
Hand on your life
Feel the rhythm of time
Hand on your life
Feel the rhythm of time.

Michael Rosen

Poetry
Night Mail

This is the Night Mail crossing the border,
Bringing the cheque and the postal order,
Letters for the rich, letters for the poor,
The shop at the corner, the girl next door.
Pulling up Beattock, a steady climb:
The gradient's against her, but she's on time.
Past cotton-grass and moorland boulder
Shovelling white steam over her shoulder,
Snorting noisily as she passes
Silent miles of wind-bent grasses.
Birds turn their heads as she approaches,
Stare from the bushes at her blank-faced coaches.
Sheep-dogs cannot turn her course;
They slumber on with paws across.
In the farm she passes no one wakes,
But a jug in the bedroom gently shakes.

Dawn freshens, Her climb is done.
Down towards Glasgow she descends,
Towards the steam tugs yelping down the glade of cranes,
Towards the fields of apparatus, the furnaces
Set on the dark plain like gigantic chessmen.
All Scotland waits for her:
In the dark glens, beside the pale-green sea lochs
Men long for news.

Letters of thanks, letters from banks,
Letters of joy from the girl and the boy,
Receipted bills and invitations
To inspect new stock to visit relations,
And applications for situations,
And timid lovers' declarations,
And gossip, gossip from all the nations,
News circumstantial, news financial,
Letters with holiday snaps to enlarge in,
Letters with faces scrawled in the margin,
Letters from uncles, cousins, and aunts,
Letters to Scotland from the South of France,
Letters of condolence to Highlands and Lowlands
Notes from overseas to Hebrides
Written on paper of every hue,
The pink, the violet, the white and the blue,
The chatty, the catty, the boring, the adoring,
The cold and official and the heart's outpouring,
Clever, stupid, short and long,
The typed and the printed and the spelt all wrong.

Thousands are still asleep
Dreaming of terrifying monsters,
Or of friendly tea beside the band at Cranston's or Crawford's:
Asleep in working Glasgow, asleep in well-set Edinburgh,
Asleep in granite Aberdeen,
They continue their dreams,
But shall wake soon and long for letters,
And none will hear the postman's knock
Without a quickening of the heart,
For who can bear to feel himself forgotten?

W.H. Auden

Non-fiction

Magic Tricks

Magic matchsticks

We are all intrigued by magicians, who seem to be able to perform impossible acts, such as pulling white rabbits out of hats and cutting a woman in half. Like all performances, though, a magician's real secret is in rehearsing thoroughly before showing anyone their tricks.

Here is a trick for you to learn. After you have practised thoroughly, try it on your family.

You will need

- several matchsticks

- a handkerchief with hems along the edges

What to do

1. Show the audience a matchstick.

2. Take a clean cotton handkerchief from your pocket, shake it out, showing both sides to prove you are not hiding anything.

3. Wrap the matchstick in the handkerchief.

4. Ask one of the audience members to feel the matchstick inside the handkerchief, and to break it.

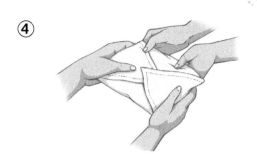

5. Shake the handkerchief, allowing the unbroken matchstick to fall onto the floor!

The secret

Before you begin the performance, slip a matchstick into the hem of the handkerchief. When you ask someone to break the wrapped-up matchstick, make sure that they break the one hidden in the hem (when they feel it, they will think it is the one they saw you wrap in the handkerchief).

It's a good idea to have two or three kerchiefs with matchsticks already secretly in the hems, as your audience is bound to be flabbergasted and ask you to do the trick again. But don't let them realise that you are changing the handkerchief, or they may become suspicious!

Non-fiction

Coin Magic

Magic coin trick

You will need:

- a ten-pence coin.

Follow these simple steps to make a coin vanish in front of your audience's eyes!

Step 1:

Hold a ten-pence coin in your hand using your forefinger and thumb.

Step 2:

Pass the coin from hand to hand.

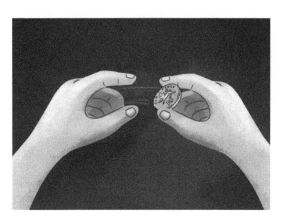

Step 3:

Here's where you do the trick: rather than passing the coin to your other hand, you use your forefinger in your empty left hand to tap the coin into your right hand.

Step 4:

Pretend you are grabbing the coin with your left hand as you are actually grasping it into your right hand. Your audience will think it has disappeared!

Non-fiction

From **How to be an Ancient Greek (I)**
by Scoular Anderson

Stage 5: No pain – no gain!

Sparta was another powerful city and rival to Athens. The Spartans prided themselves on having an almost unbeatable army. This was because warriors spent most of their lives in military training.

For this, the Spartans wanted only healthy men so when a boy was born, he was examined by government officials for any sign of weakness. If the baby failed to pass this inspection, he was left on a mountainside to die.

If you were a strong and healthy boy you trained to be a soldier from an early age. At seven, boys joined one of the military clubs in the city. From then until retirement age, they lived in the army barracks. When they married, they were only allowed out on short visits to see their wives and families.

Spartan army training was very harsh. The young soldiers had to withstand beatings to prove how strong they were. They were sent out to live rough in the countryside. They had no food, shoes or proper clothes, only a knife and a cloak.

The cheese test

Young recruits had to run along the front of a temple gathering as many bits of cheese as they could – and dodging men with whips. Some boys died from their wounds.

Ouch!

Spartan girls went into training, too. They had to take part in various sports so they would become healthy women and have strong babies – who would become good soldiers.

Unlike the Athenians, the Spartans had no time for the theatre, poetry or history – all the men were too busy training. Both Athens and Sparta wanted to be the most powerful city in the area and they eventually went to war. The war lasted 27 years and left both sides ruined.

Non-fiction

From **How to be an Ancient Greek (2)**
by Scoular Anderson

Stage 14: Work up a sweat

As an Ancient Greek, you like to keep really fit. A young Greek man needed a strong body for fighting in battle. Exercise is also a way of pleasing the gods so every few years big sports festivals were held. The games took place at special sports grounds. There was always a temple in the middle of the **complex** and all around were training areas, running tracks, meeting rooms and hotels for officials.

People travelled great distances to take part and the most popular games were those at Olympia.

If you won an event, all you were given was a **wreath** to place on your head. However, when you got home, you were treated as a hero and given money or even free food for life.

Women were not allowed to take part or even watch the events, so they held their own games which were known as the Heraia in honour of the goddess Hera.

As an athlete, you had to pay for a trainer, equipment and travel. You didn't have to buy clothes as you performed naked! If you didn't obey the rules you would feel the sting of the referee's cane on your back.

The Games Events

Boxing
The match went on until one of the boxers was knocked unconscious. The contest could last for hours.

Chariot racing

This event was very dangerous and accidents were common.

Running

There were races of various lengths including one where the runners wore full battle armour.

The Pentathlon

This consisted of five events: running, wrestling, jumping and throwing the discus and javelin. Jumpers often held weights when they swung their arms. This helped them jump further.

The Trojan War

Troy was one of the greatest cities in the ancient world. It was surrounded by mighty walls, so huge they were considered impenetrable.

One day a Trojan prince called Paris travelled to Greece to meet the king, Menelaus, and Helen, his wife, who was undoubtedly the most beautiful woman he had ever set eyes on. Paris fell deeply in love with her and asked her to return to Troy with him. Initially Helen refused, but eventually Paris persuaded her, and they secretly eloped while Menelaus was away.

It is not difficult to imagine the king's bewilderment and anger when he returned. He sent his messengers to ask the Trojans to ensure the immediate return of Helen to Greece. When they refused he brought together his best ships and bravest soldiers under the command of Agamemnon, his brother. It was thus that the Trojan War started.

Achilles

Legend has it that one of the great Greek heroes of the Trojan War was Achilles, a half-god, being the son of Zeus, the Greeks' most important god.

When he was a baby, Achilles' mother had dipped him in the magic waters of the Styx River. This meant every part of his body was thus protected from harm, except the heel by which his mother had held him when she dangled him in the waters. Achilles grew to become a strong, powerful soldier who could fight any battle, and without fear of ever being wounded!

One such battle led to the death of Paris's younger brother, Hector, but eventually Paris brought his revenge. One day, when Achilles was kneeling at prayer, Paris shot a poisoned arrow into his heel, killing the hitherto invincible hero. To this day, people talk of someone's Achilles' heel, meaning his or her weak point.

The Trojan Horse

Neither side seemed to be getting the upper hand in the conflict. In desperation, the Greek hero Odysseus devised a plan to build a huge wooden statue of a horse and leave it as a religious offering. Unbeknown to the Trojans, Greek warriors hid inside the hollow statue. The other Greeks sailed away from Troy.

Delighted with the apparent retreat of their enemy, the Trojans opened the gates and flocked out of their city. As they were celebrating they came across the horse. Intrigued, they poked it and tapped it, and then found Sinon, a Greek soldier, hiding nearby.

They forced him, or so they thought, to divulge the secret of the horse. Sinon said that if the Trojans 'captured' the horse, the Greeks would be so demoralised they would never return to Troy again.

The Trojans were delighted! The strongest man heaved and dragged the wooden monster into the city, needing to destroy part of the city wall in the process as it wouldn't fit through even the widest gate. That night there was a great celebration in Troy with feasts and dancing, and lots of liquor! Later, with everyone exhausted and sleeping soundly, Sinon crept up to the huge horse and released the Greek soldiers. Then he ran to open all the city gates to let in the other Greek soldiers, whose boats had returned under the cover of dark.

It was a rout! The Greek's destroyed the Trojan army before it could properly gather itself, and set fire to the city. Helen was taken captive and forced to return to King Menelaus, and the long, bloody, Trojan War ended.

Fiction

From **The Golden Turtle** by Gervaise Phinn

Kobayashi Issei was a poor fisherman who fished the clear waters in his old leaky rowing boat near the small island of Tsunoshima, catching just enough to feed himself and his family. The other fishermen, with their large strong nets and fast new boats, would catch all the biggest and the tastiest fish. They laughed at Kobayashi Issei in his old leaky rowing boat as they sped past him for the open sea, riding the waves, sails billowing in the wind.

But the young fisherman did not mind. He smiled and waved, then cast his net and sang to himself. He loved the open sea, the taste of salt on his lips and the warmth of the sun on his face. Kobayashi Issei wanted nothing more than his small boat and a few fish each day to feed him and his family.

One day, his net sank beneath the boat. It was as if a great weight was pulling it down. Kobayashi Issei tugged and heaved, but, try as he might, he could not raise the net. All day he struggled, sweating and panting, but to no avail. As the sun began to set he tied the net to the stern of the boat and began to row with all his strength.

He had never pulled so hard on the oars. The boards creaked and the water leaked in, but he rowed and rowed. It was a slow, painful journey, but finally he pulled into the small harbour, still with the heavy weight in his net below the boat.

The other fishermen had sold their catches and they watched with interest as Kobayashi Issei struggled and strained to pull his boat up the sandy shore.

Then they laughed until they cried as the young fisherman tried to heave the net from the water, slipping and tripping and falling in the sand.

"Caught a whale, have you, Kobayashi Issei?" the fishermen mocked.

"Or a sunken treasure?"

"Or a harvest of seaweed?"

"Or rocks?"

But they stopped laughing and gasped when they saw what was in the net.

It was a turtle, but no ordinary turtle. The creature's shell was a bright yellow and shone in the sunlight like plates of polished gold. Its head was huge and wrinkled and its large black eyes glinted fiercely. The fishermen ran to the shore as Kobayashi Issei pulled the huge creature up the sand.

"What a catch!" the fishermen cried.

"It must be worth a small fortune."

"Think of all the turtle soup."

"And the shell – what a price that will fetch!"

Now, Kobayashi Issei was a kind-hearted man. As he pulled away the tangle of net, the turtle stared up at him. Its eyes were no longer flashing, but looked large and sad and its beak of a mouth opened wide as it gasped for air.

Kobayashi Issei did not think twice. He turned the turtle to face the water and pushed. He pushed and pushed until the creature was very nearly at the lip of the sea.

"What are you doing?" cried the fishermen.

"He's letting it go."

"He must be mad!"

"Stop him someone!"

As the people clustered around him, Kobayashi Issei stood and faced them.

"Is this my turtle?" he asked.

"It is," they replied.

"And did I not catch it with my own hands in my own net in my own boat?"

"You did," they cried.

"And can I do what I wish with this turtle?"

"You can," they told him.

"Then I shall return it to the ocean from where it came."

79

With one great heave, he pushed the creature into the water and watched it dive into the depths.

"What a fool!" the fishermen cried.

"All the money he could have had for the shell."

"And enough turtle soup to eat for a year."

It was exactly a year later as Kobayashi Issei in his old leaky rowing boat watched as the fishermen sped past him for the open sea. He smiled and waved, then cast his net and sang to himself.

As the sun set and he headed for home, Kobayashi Issei heard a voice calling him.

"Taro! Taro!" it called.

The young fisherman was greatly afraid and he trembled with fear.

"Who is it who calls me?" he asked timidly.

"Taro!" came the voice again. "It is I."

Kobayashi Issei peered nervously over the side of his boat. Swimming slowly alongside was the golden-shelled turtle.

"You are a good-hearted man, Kobayashi Issei. It was you who returned me to the sea when you had caught me in your net. It was you who saved my life when others would have killed me. Come with me, Kobayashi Issei, to the kingdom beneath the sea and you will see such wonders that no man has ever seen and have such riches that no man has ever possessed. Do not be afraid, for I will take great care of you."

So Kobayashi Issei slipped over the side of his boat and, climbing onto the turtle's golden shell and clinging tightly, he sank beneath the sea and was taken deep down to the depths of the cold blue ocean. And there in a palace of crimson coral and sparkling crystal, on a carpet of silver pearls and golden amber, he saw riches beyond his wildest dreams and such wonders that no man had ever seen: gleaming sharks as big as boats, great green octopuses with arms as thick as tree trunks, giant crabs with enormous claws, lobsters the size of houses and millions of tiny silver fish like slivers of glittering glass.

"Stay here with us, Kobayashi Issei," said the turtle, "and you shall have everything you could ever wish for. You will never need to fish again in your old leaky boat or be laughed at by the fishermen. Stay here in the kingdom beneath the sea."

"I cannot," replied the young fisherman, "for I would long for my home and I would miss my leaky old boat. I have a wife and children waiting for me and I would be lonely here. All the riches of the ocean floor and all the wonderful sights I would see could never mean more to me than my home and family."

"Very well," said the turtle, "if that is your wish, but take with you pocketfuls of pearls and amber, corals and crystals and become the richest man in your village. For you have been kind, Kobayashi Issei, and I wish to reward you."

"I thank you," said Kobayashi Issei, "but kindness is its own reward. It costs nothing to give and is a treasure to receive. I have no need of all your riches."

The turtle swam to the surface with Kobayashi Issei clinging tightly to his golden shell and watched as the fisherman sailed for home.

And from that day to this, Kobayashi Issei's net was never empty. When the sea was rough, it swelled with fish. When the sea was calm, it bulged. In winter and summer alike Kobayashi Issei returned with the biggest and the finest catch.

When times became bleak on the small island of Tsunoshima and the sea seemed empty and the other fishermen made for home with nothing in their nets and with sad hearts, Kobayashi Issei always sailed home with a boat bursting with fish. The fishermen who had laughed at him felt ashamed, for Kobayashi Issei, a good-hearted man, shared his good fortune with all.

Fiction

Shen Nung

China's age of the 'Great Ten' was when each of ten successive emperors brought new skills and knowledge to this great civilisation, but none more so than Shen Nung. Some legends say he had the head of an ox, but the body of a man. Being part ox, led him to invent the plough, which in China was always pulled by oxen. He showed his people how then to sow seeds and cultivate crops.

He also taught them how to tame the forests and turn thickly overgrown woodlands into productive land. If they felled the trees in a small area and burned the stumps, they could plant their crops more easily. The ash would enrich the soil, helping their crops to grow well.

Shen Nung is also remembered as the god of medicine. He showed the people which plants would heal them when they were sick. According to the stories he was said to have a see-through stomach which enabled him to watch what was happening inside his body as he ate strange plants. One day he boiled some rare leaves and made a sort of vegetable stew. He drank the juice he strained from the mix. He had discovered tea!

Another of his useful discoveries was ginseng, a plant whose roots clean the blood of any impurities. It was soon recognised as a tonic, making tired people feel energetic and older people feel younger.

Sadly, Shen Nung grew careless and eventually died after swallowing a strange form of grass that was so sharp it cut his stomach to ribbons. But by then the great Emperor had discovered and invented so much his reputation was certain to live on for generations to come.

But so too was Shen Nung's wife to be remembered. She had mastered the art of breeding silkworms.
This is a skill known as sericulture. Silkworms produce a thread that can be woven into silk cloth, for which the Chinese have ever since been renowned. To this day much of the best silk in the world comes from China. Shen Nung's wife was also deified, and became the goddess of housecrafts.

Medicine, tea, farming and fine cloth helped make China into one of the greatest civilisations the world has known – and dating back from a time several thousands of years ago, when people in most Western countries were still living in very primitive conditions.

Non-fiction

Barack Obama: A Biography

Barack Hussein Obama was born on 4 August 1961, in Honolulu, Hawaii. Obama's mother, Ann Dunham, grew up in Kansas, USA, and his father, Barack Obama, Sr, was born in Nyanza Province, Kenya. They met at the University of Hawaii and married on 2 February 1961.

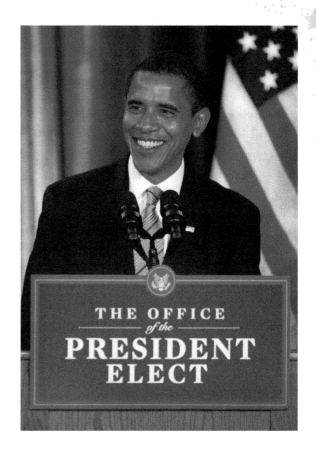

Obama's parents separated when he was only two years old, and later divorced. Obama, Sr went on to Harvard University to pursue further studies, and then returned to Kenya in 1965. In 1966, Barack's mother married Lolo Soetoro and the family moved to Indonesia. Several incidents in Indonesia left Barack's mother afraid for her son's safety and education so, at the age of ten, he was sent back to Hawaii to live with his maternal grandparents. His mother and half-sister later joined them.

While living with his grandparents, Obama was given a place a place in the highly regarded Punahou Academy, where he excelled in basketball. As one of only three black students at the school, Obama became conscious of racism and what it meant to be African-American. He later described how he struggled to reconcile other people's perceptions of his multiracial heritage with his own sense of himself.

"I began to notice there was nobody like me in the Christmas catalogues … and that Santa was a white man," he said.

Obama was also unhappy because of the absence of his father. His father wrote to him regularly but, though he travelled around the world on official business for Kenya, he only visited once. Obama, Jr. was 22 years old when he received the news that his father had died in a car accident in Kenya.

Obama attended Colombia University and found New York's racial tension inescapable. He attended Harvard Law School and chose to practise civil-rights law in Chicago. He represented victims of housing and employment discrimination and worked on voting-rights legislation. He married Michelle Robinson, a fellow attorney. His district included some of the poorest ghettos on the South Side.

In 2004, Obama was elected to the US Senate as a Democrat. He gained national attention by giving a rousing and well-received speech at the Democratic National Convention. In 2008 he ran for President and won. In January 2009, he was sworn in as the 44th President of the United States, the first African-American ever elected to that position.

From Walter Tull: Footballer, Soldier, Hero
by Dan Lyndon

The Battle of the Somme

On 1 July 1916 one of the most important battles of the First World War began in an area of France known as the Somme. The British Generals who planned the battle were confident that they would be able to defeat the German Army quickly and easily, but they were wrong.

The British soldiers had to walk through an area called No Man's Land, a strip of land that separated the Allies from the Germans. Walter had to dodge machine-gun bullets and barbed wire, deep trenches made by exploding shells and the bodies of soldiers who had been killed.

On the very first day of the battle there were over 50,000 British soldiers killed and wounded. After three weeks of fighting at the Somme, Walter and the rest of the Middlesex Regiment were told to move back to the rear to get a well-deserved break from the fighting.

The Battle of the Somme lasted for five months and hundreds of men on both sides were killed. By the time the battle was over in November 1916, over one and a half million men had been killed or wounded in the fighting. Of the 400 men of Walter's Middlesex Regiment who went fighting, only 79 returned.

Officer Class

Walter arrived back in England on Boxing Day 1916, the first time that he'd been given leave since joining the Army. Walter had been recommended by Lieutenant Colonel Haig Brown to take part in an officer training course in Scotland. There were two other black officers in the British Army, but they were in the Medical units and did not command other soldiers. Walter's inclusion on the course showed a significant change in attitude towards black people by the Army even though this was not officially recognised.

During four months of training, Walter learnt how to train and command groups of soldiers, how to attack and defend against the enemy and how to read maps. He also learnt how to throw grenades and build trenches. All of these were vital skills that soldiers needed to use, but officers also needed to learn how to organise and manage large groups of men and support them in very dangerous situations.

The trainee officers were given manuals that covered in great detail all the different scenarios that they would have to deal with. This ranged from setting up a machine-gun post, to using pigeons to send secret messages.

As part of the training, every trainee would be tested to make sure that they knew everything in the manual. Walter also needed to demonstrate **initiative** and leadership and show a great deal of self-confidence. He took his exams at the end of May and graduated on 29 May 1917.

Walter became the first black Infantry Officer in the history of the British Army. This was an amazing event as the official Army law said that officers had to be of, "pure European descent" and Walter's father had come from the Caribbean. Walter's strength of character and his leadership talents meant that he was rewarded with a promotion despite Army law. Walter was the first black officer to take command of white soldiers and lead them into battle, when it would have been very shocking to some people, who still believed that black people were inferior to white people.

Walter returned from France in August 1917 and rejoined the Middlesex Regiment, where he was given his first group of soldiers to command. There were some advantages to being an officer. Walter was given four meals a day instead of three, he was paid more and could take more leave. However, with these privileges came with the responsibility of looking after his men. Walter used his experiences of playing professional football to make sure that his soldiers became part of a new team, one where the men looked out for each other when they were going into battle.